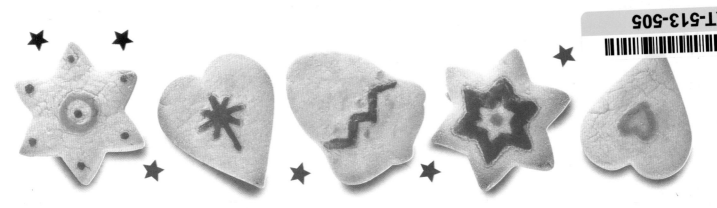

CHRISTMAS COOKING

Rebecca Gilpin and Catherine Atkinson

Edited by Fiona Watt
Designed by Amanda Gulliver
Photographs by Howard Allman
Illustrated by Kim Lane and Sue Stitt

Managing Designer: Mary Cartwright
With thanks to Katrina Fearn and Brian Voakes

Contents

Little Christmas trees

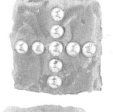

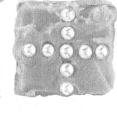

To make 10 trees and 16 presents, you will need:
275g (9½ oz) self-raising flour
225g (8oz) soft margarine
4 tablespoons milk
1 level teaspoon of baking powder
225g (8oz) caster sugar
2-3 drops vanilla essence
4 medium eggs

For the butter icing:
75g (3oz) butter, softened
175g (6oz) icing sugar
2 teaspoons lemon juice
food dyes

You could arrange the presents around the trees.

Heat the oven to 180°C, 350°F, gas mark 4, before you start.

Use a roasting tin.

Use a paper towel to wipe oil on the tin.

Use a wooden spoon.

1. Draw around a tin on greaseproof paper. Cut it out. Wipe oil inside the tin. Put the paper into the tin and oil the paper.

2. Sift the flour into a large mixing bowl. Add the margarine, milk, baking powder, sugar and vanilla essence.

3. Break the eggs into a small bowl. Beat them with a fork. Add them to the flour mixture. Beat everything together well.

Make trunks for the trees from chocolate bars or biscuits.

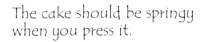

The cake should be springy when you press it.

4. Spoon the mixture into the tin. Smooth the top. Bake it in the oven for 40-45 minutes, until the middle is springy.

5. Leave the cake in the tin to cool, then lift it out. Put the butter into a bowl. Beat it with a wooden spoon until it is creamy.

6. Sift in the icing sugar and stir it in, a little at a time. Stir in the lemon juice. Put three-quarters of the icing in a bowl.

To make the colour stronger, add more dye, a drop at a time.

These will be the presents.

7. Mix in a little green food dye. Divide the rest of the icing into three bowls. Mix a drop of food dye into each one.

8. Cut a strip 7cm (3in) wide from one end of the cake. Cut it into 16 small squares. Cut the cake in half along its length.

9. Cut out ten triangles. Ice them with green icing. Ice the presents with the other icing. Press sweets onto the cakes.

Decorate the trees with sweets.

Coconut mice

To make about eight large mice, five medium
mice and three baby mice, you will need:
250g (9oz) icing sugar, sifted
200g (8oz) tin of condensed milk
175g (7oz) desiccated coconut
red food dye
sweets for ears
silver cake-decorating balls
liquorice 'bootlaces'

1. Mix the icing sugar
and the condensed milk
together in a bowl. Mix
in the coconut. Put the
mixture into two bowls.

2. Add a few drops of
red dye to each bowl
and mix it in. Then add a
few more drops of dye to
one of the bowls.

*For baby mice,
use a teaspoon
for the body.*

3. Dip a clean tablespoon into some water and let it drip. Then, lift out a big spoonful of the mixture.

4. Pat the spoonful smooth on top. Turn the spoon over and put the shape onto a piece of plastic foodwrap.

5. Pinch a nose at the thinner end of the spoon shape. Then, add sweets for ears and silver balls for eyes.

6. Push a piece of liquorice under the shape, as a tail. Leave the mouse to harden on a plate. Make more mice.

Use a dessertspoon for a medium mouse.

Cheesy Christmas stars

To make about 25 stars, you will need:
150g (6oz) self-raising flour
half a teaspoon of salt
75g (3oz) butter or margarine
75g (3oz) cheese, finely grated
1 egg and 1 tablespoon of milk, beaten together
a star-shaped cutter
a greased baking sheet

Heat the oven to 200°C, 400°F, gas mark 6,
before you start.

1. Sift the flour and salt through a sieve. Add the butter or margarine and rub it with your fingers to make fine crumbs.

2. Leave a tablespoon of the grated cheese on a saucer. Add the rest of the cheese to the bowl and stir it in.

3. Put a tablespoon of the beaten egg and milk mixture into a cup. Mix the rest into the flour to make a dough.

Use a rolling pin.

Use a pastry brush.

4. Sprinkle flour onto a clean work surface. Roll out the dough, until it is slightly thinner than your little finger.

5. Use the cutter to cut out star shapes. Cut them close together. Make the scraps into a ball, and roll them out.

6. Cut out more stars. Brush the stars with the rest of the egg mixture, then sprinkle them with the rest of the cheese.

7. Put the stars onto the greased baking sheet. Bake them in the oven for eight to ten minutes, until they are golden.

These stars are delicious to eat when they are warm.

Creamy chocolate fudge

To make about 36 squares of fudge, you will need:
75g (3oz) full-fat cream cheese
350g (12oz) icing sugar
1 level tablespoon of cocoa powder
1 teaspoon of oil, for wiping
75g (3oz) plain chocolate drops
40g (1½oz) butter
a shallow 15cm (6in) square cake tin
greaseproof paper

Find out how to wrap
pieces of fudge on page 30.

Use a pencil to draw around the tin.

1. Put the cream cheese into a bowl. Sift the icing sugar and cocoa through a sieve into the bowl too. Mix them together well.

2. Put the cake tin onto a sheet of greaseproof paper and draw around it. Cut out the shape, just inside the line.

3. Use a paper towel to wipe oil onto the sides and base of the tin. Press in the paper square and wipe it too.

4. Melt the chocolate and butter as in steps 1-3 on page 20. Then, stir in a tablespoon of the cream cheese mixture.

5. Pour the chocolate into the cheese mixture in the bowl. Beat them together with a spoon until they are creamy.

6. Spoon the mixture into the tin, and push it into the corners. Make the top of the fudge as flat as you can.

7. Smooth the top of the fudge with the back of a spoon. Put the tin in the fridge for two hours, or until the fudge is firm.

8. Use a blunt knife to loosen the edges of the fudge, then turn it out onto a large plate. Remove the paper.

9. Cut the fudge into lots of squares. Then, put the plate in the fridge for two hours, until the fudge is hard.

Crinkly Christmas pies

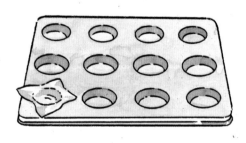

To make 12 pies, you will need:
4 eating apples
3 tablespoons orange juice or cold water
50g (2oz) dried cranberries or sultanas
2 teaspoons caster sugar
half a teaspoon of ground cinnamon
100g (4oz) filo pastry (about 6 sheets)
50g (2oz) butter
2 teaspoons icing sugar
a baking tray with shallow pans or 12-hole muffin tin

Heat the oven to 190°C, 375°F, gas mark 5, before you start.

You may need to ask someone to help you.

1. Peel the apples. Cut them into quarters and cut out the cores. Cut them into small pieces and put them in the pan.

Put the lid back on after you've stirred the apples.

2. Add the juice or water and put the pan on a very low heat. Cover it with a lid. Cook for 20 minutes, stirring often.

Stir the mixture often.

3. Stir in the fruit, caster sugar and cinnamon. Cook the mixture for about five minutes, then take it off the heat.

Keep the six sheets together.

4. Take the pan off the heat. Unwrap the pastry. Cut all the sheets into six squares. Cover them with foodwrap.

Use a pastry brush.

5. Put the butter in a small pan and melt it over a low heat. Brush a little butter over one of the pastry squares.

6. Put the square into a hole in the tray, buttered side up. Press it gently into the hole. Brush butter onto another square.

Overlap the pastry sheets so that they look like a star.

7. Put this square over the first one. Overlap the corners slightly. Butter and add a third square. Repeat in all the holes.

Heat the apples until they bubble a little.

Eat the pies warm or cold.

8. Put the tray on the middle shelf of the oven and cook for 10 minutes. Take it out and leave it to cool for five minutes.

9. Take the pastry cases out of the tray and put them onto a large plate. Heat the apples again for about two minutes.

10. Spoon the apple mixture into the pastry cases, so that they are almost full. Sift icing sugar onto them.

Painted biscuits

To make about 15 biscuits, you will need:
50g (2oz) icing sugar
75g (3oz) soft margarine
the yolk from a large egg
vanilla essence
150g (5oz) plain flour
plastic foodwrap
big cutters
a greased baking sheet

To decorate the biscuits:
an egg yolk
food dyes

Heat the oven to 180°C, 350°F, gas mark 4, before you start.

Use a wooden spoon.

1. Sift the icing sugar through a sieve into a large bowl. Add the margarine and mix well until they are smooth.

2. Add the large egg yolk and stir it in well. Then, add a few drops of vanilla essence. Stir the vanilla into the mixture.

3. Hold a sieve over the bowl and pour the flour into it. Sift the flour through the sieve, to remove any lumps.

4. Mix in the flour until you get a smooth dough. Wrap the dough in plastic foodwrap and put it in the freezer.

Decorate your biscuits with lots of different patterns.

It takes time to decorate the biscuits, so you could freeze some of the dough to use another day.

5. Put the egg yolk into a bowl and beat it with a fork. Put it onto saucers. Mix a few drops of food dye into each one.

6. Take the dough out of the freezer. Roll out half of it onto a floury work surface, until it is as thin as your little finger.

7. Press out shapes with cutters. Use a fish slice to lift them onto a baking sheet. Roll out the rest of the dough.

8. Cut out more shapes. Use a clean paintbrush to paint shapes on the biscuits with the egg and dye mixture.

9. Bake the biscuits for 10-12 minutes. Remove them from the oven. Let them cool a little, then lift them onto a wire rack.

Starry jam tart

To make one jam tart, you will need:
350g (12oz) packet shortcrust pastry
about 2 tablespoons plain flour
6 rounded tablespoons seedless raspberry or
strawberry jam
1 tablespoon of milk
20cm (8in) fluted flan tin
a small star-shaped cutter

Heat the oven to 200°C, 400°F, gas mark 6, before you start.

You can use any shape of cutter you like. Stars and holly leaves look very Christmassy.

1. Take the pastry out of the fridge and leave it for 10 minutes. Sprinkle a clean work surface with some flour.

2. Cut off quarter of the pastry and wrap it in some plastic foodwrap. Sprinkle some flour onto a rolling pin.

Sift a slice of tart with a little icing sugar and serve it with cream.

The rolling pin cuts off the extra pastry.

3. Roll out the bigger piece of pastry. Turn it a little, then roll it again. Make a circle about 30cm (12in) across.

4. Put the rolling pin at one side of the pastry. Roll the pastry around it and lift it up. Place it over the tin and unroll it.

5. Dip a finger into some flour and press the pastry into the edges of the tin. Then, roll the rolling pin across the top.

6. Spoon the jam into the pastry case. Spread it out with the back of a spoon. Roll out the other quarter of the pastry.

7. Using the cutter, cut out about 12 pastry shapes. Brush them with a little milk and place them on top of the jam.

The pastry should be golden brown.

8. Put the jam tart in the oven. Bake it for about 20 minutes. Take the tart from the oven and let the jam cool before serving.

Peppermint creams

To make about 25 peppermint creams, you will need:
250g (9oz) icing sugar
half the white of a small egg, mixed from dried
egg white (mix as directed on the packet)
1 teaspoon peppermint flavouring
2 teaspoons lemon juice
green food dye
a rolling pin
small cutters
a baking sheet covered in
plastic foodwrap

Put peppermint
creams in boxes, to
give as presents.

1. Sift the icing sugar through a sieve into a large bowl. Make a hole in the middle of the sugar with a spoon.

2. Mix the egg white, peppermint flavouring and lemon juice in a small bowl. Pour the mixture into the sugar.

3. Use a blunt knife to stir the mixture. Then, squeeze it between your fingers until it is smooth, like a dough.

4. Cut the mixture into two pieces. Put each piece into a bowl. Add a few drops of green food dye to one bowl.

5. Use your fingers to mix in the dye. If the mixture is sticky, add a little more icing sugar and mix it in.

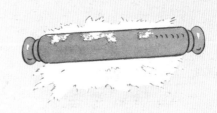

6. Sprinkle a little icing sugar onto a clean work surface. Sprinkle some onto a rolling pin too, to stop the mixture sticking.

Cut the shapes close together.

7. Roll out the green mixture until it is about as thick as your little finger. Use cutters to cut out lots of shapes.

8. Use a blunt knife to lift the shapes onto the baking sheet. Roll out the white mixture and cut out more shapes.

9. Lift all the shapes onto the baking sheet. Leave them for at least an hour until they become hard.

Shortbread

To make eight pieces, you will need:
butter for greasing
150g (5oz) plain flour
25g (1oz) rice flour or ground rice
100g (4oz) butter, refrigerated, cut into chunks
50g (2oz) caster sugar
a 20cm (8in) shallow round tin

Heat the oven to 150°C, 300°F, gas mark 2, before you start.

1. Grease the bottom and sides of the tin with some butter on a piece of paper towel. Make sure it is all greased.

2. Sift the flour and rice flour or ground rice through a sieve into a large bowl. Add the butter to the bowl.

3. Mix in the butter so that it is coated in flour. Rub it into the flour with your fingers until it is like fine breadcrumbs.

4. Stir in the sugar with a wooden spoon. Hold the bowl with one hand and squeeze the mixture into a ball with the other.

5. Press the mixture into the tin with your fingers. Use the back of a spoon to smooth the top and make it level.

6. Use a fork to press patterns around the edge and holes in the middle. Cut the shortbread into eight pieces.

Shortbread makes an ideal present. See pages 30-31 for wrapping ideas.

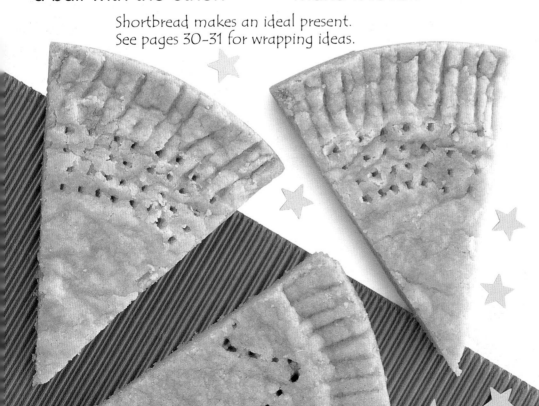

7. Bake the shortbread for 30 minutes, until it is golden. After 10 minutes, take it out of the tin. Put it on a wire rack to cool.

Chocolate truffles

To make about 10 truffles, you will need:
100g (4oz) plain or white chocolate drops
25g (1oz) butter
25g (1oz) icing sugar
50g (2oz) plain cake, crumbled into fine crumbs
2 tablespoons desiccated coconut
2 tablespoons chocolate sugar strands
small paper cases for sweets

1. Pour water into a pan, until it is about 3cm (1in) deep. Heat it until it bubbles, then remove the pan from the heat.

2. Put the chocolate drops and the butter into a heatproof bowl. Put on oven gloves and gently put the bowl in the pan.

Ask someone to help you to lift the bowl.

3. Stir the chocolate and butter together until they have melted. Using oven gloves, carefully lift the bowl out of the water.

4. Sift the icing sugar through a sieve into the chocolate. Add the cake crumbs and stir until everything is well mixed.

The white truffles are covered with desiccated coconut.

5. Leave the mixture to cool. Put the desiccated coconut onto one plate, and the chocolate strands onto another.

6. When the mixture is firm and thick, scoop up some with a teaspoon. Put the spoonful into the coconut or strands.

Roll the spoonful to make a ball.

7. Roll the spoonful of chocolate around until it is covered, then put it in a paper case. Make lots more truffles.

8. Put the truffles onto a large plate. Put the plate in the fridge for 30 minutes, or until the truffles are firm.

Shining star biscuits

To make about 20 biscuits, you will need:
50g (2oz) light soft brown sugar
50g (2oz) butter, softened
a small egg
115g (4½oz) plain flour
15g (½oz) cornflour
1 teaspoon ground mixed spice
solid boiled sweets
a large star-shaped cutter
a fat drinking straw
a small round cutter, slightly bigger than the sweets
a large baking tray lined with baking parchment

Heat the oven to 180°C, 350°F, gas mark 4, before you start.

Thread thin ribbon through the holes.

1. Using a wooden spoon, mix the sugar and butter really well, getting rid of any lumps in the mixture.

2. Break the egg into a separate bowl. Beat the egg with a fork until the yolk and the white are mixed together.

3. Mix half of the beaten egg into the mixture in the bowl, a little at a time. You don't need the other half.

4. Sift the flour, cornflour and mixed spice through a sieve. Mix everything together really well with a wooden spoon.

5. Squeeze the mixture with your hands until a firm dough is formed. Make the dough into a large ball.

6. Sprinkle a clean work surface with a little flour. Then, roll out the ball of dough until it is 5mm (¼ in) thick.

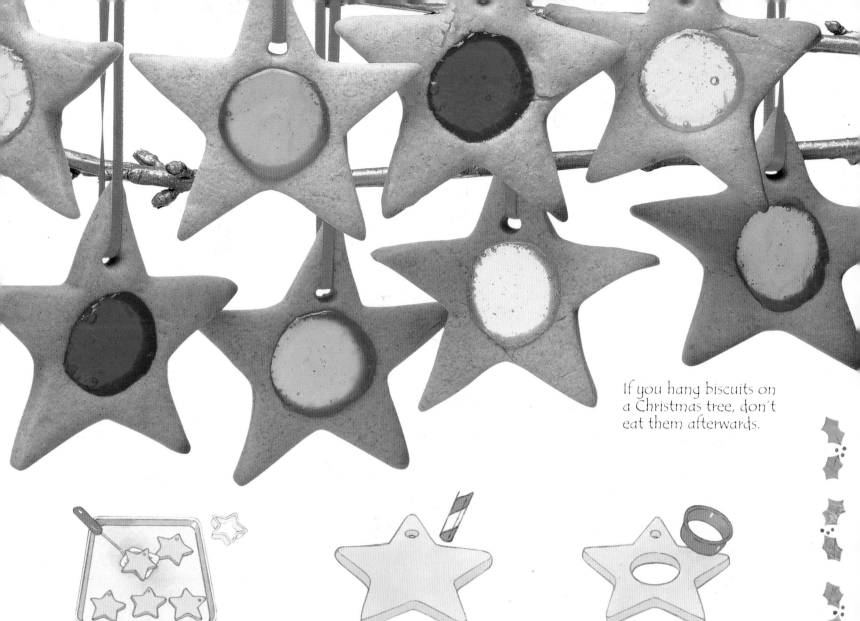

If you hang biscuits on a Christmas tree, don't eat them afterwards.

7. Line the baking tray. Use a large cutter to press out lots of stars. Use a fish slice to put them onto the tray.

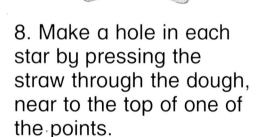

8. Make a hole in each star by pressing the straw through the dough, near to the top of one of the points.

9. Use a small round cutter to cut a hole in the middle of each star. The hole should be slightly bigger than the sweet.

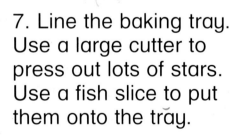

10. Squeeze the leftover pieces of dough into a ball. Roll them out. Cut out more stars. Put them on the baking tray.

11. Drop a sweet into the hole in the middle of each star shape. Put the baking tray on the middle shelf of the oven.

12. Bake the shapes for twelve minutes, then take them out. Leave them on the baking tray until they are cold.

Snowmen and presents

To make lots of snowmen
and presents, you will need:
250g (9oz) 'white' marzipan*
green, red and yellow
food dyes
toothpicks

Colouring marzipan

Add a little icing sugar
if the marzipan gets
too sticky.

1. Unwrap the marzipan. Then, put it on a plate and cut it into quarters. Put each quarter into a small bowl.

2. Add one drop of green food dye, then mix it in with your fingers. Carry on until the marzipan is evenly coloured.

3. Leave one quarter of the marzipan 'white'. Add red food dye to one quarter, and yellow to the other. Mix in the dye.

A snowman

Put the marzipan
balls on a plate.

Press the ball
with your
thumb.

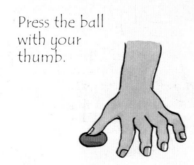

Cross the
ends of the
scarf.

1. Roll a piece of 'white' marzipan into a ball. Then, make a smaller ball. Press the smaller ball onto the larger one.

2. Roll a small ball of red marzipan. Press it to make a circle. Put it on the snowman's head. Put a tiny red ball on top.

3. Roll a thin sausage from red marzipan. Wrap it around the snowman for a scarf. Press in a face with a toothpick.

* Marzipan contains ground nuts. Don't make these if you are allergic to nuts.

Ice a cake with butter icing (see pages 2-3) and decorate it with snowmen and presents.

A present

1. Roll a ball of red marzipan and put it on a work surface. Gently press the flat side of a knife down on the ball.

2. Turn the ball on its side and press it with the knife again. Keep on doing this until the ball becomes a cube.

3. Roll thin sausages of green marzipan. Press them onto the cube, in a cross. Add two loops in the middle for a bow.

Iced gingerbread hearts

To make about 20 biscuits, you will need:
350g (12oz) plain flour
2 teaspoons ground ginger
1 teaspoon of bicarbonate of soda
100g (4oz) butter or margarine, cut into chunks
175g (6oz) soft light brown sugar
1 medium egg
4 tablespoons golden syrup
white writing icing
silver cake-decorating balls
a large heart-shaped cutter
2 greased baking trays

Heat the oven to 190°C, 375°F, gas mark 5,
before you start.

You could wrap some
biscuits in tissue paper
or cellophane twists,
to give as a present.

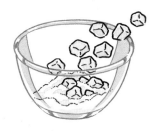  

1. Sift the flour, ground ginger and bicarbonate of soda into a large bowl. Add the butter or margarine chunks.

2. Rub the butter or margarine into the flour with your fingers until it is like fine breadcrumbs. Stir in the sugar.

3. Break the egg into a small bowl, then add the syrup. Beat well with a fork, then stir the egg mixture into the flour.

  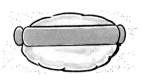

4. Mix with a metal spoon until you make a dough. Sprinkle flour onto a work surface. Put the dough on it.

5. Stretch the dough by pushing it away from you. Fold it in half and repeat. Carry on doing this until it is smooth.

6. Sprinkle more flour onto the work surface. Cut the dough in half. Roll out one half until it is 5mm (¼ in) thick.

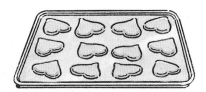  

7. Use a cutter to cut out lots of hearts. Then, lift the hearts onto the greased baking trays with a fish slice.

8. Roll out the rest of the dough and cut out more hearts. Put them on the baking trays, then put the baking trays in the oven.

9. Bake the biscuits for 12-15 minutes. They will turn golden brown. Carefully lift the baking trays from the oven.

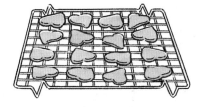  

10. Leave the biscuits on the trays for about 5 minutes. Then, lift them onto a wire rack. Leave them to cool.

11. When the biscuits are cold, draw lines across them with the icing. Cross some of the lines over each other.

12. Leave the icing to harden a little. Then, push in a silver cake-decorating ball where the lines of icing cross.

Christmas tree cakes

To make 15 cakes, you will need:
100g (4oz) self-raising flour
2 medium eggs
100g (4oz) soft margarine
100g (4oz) caster sugar
paper cake cases
2 baking trays with shallow pans
small sweets for decorating

For the butter icing:
75g (3oz) butter or margarine, softened
175g (6oz) icing sugar, sifted
2 teaspoons lemon juice or a few
drops of vanilla essence

Heat the oven to 190°C, 375°F, gas mark 5,
before you start.

1. Break the eggs into a cup. Then, sift the flour through a sieve into a big bowl. Add the eggs, margarine and sugar.

2. Stir everything together with a wooden spoon. Carry on until you get a smooth creamy mixture.

3. Put the paper cases into the pans in the baking trays. Use a spoon to half-fill each case with the mixture.

Stir it very quickly.

4. Bake the cakes for about 20 minutes and carefully take them out of the oven. Leave them on a rack to cool.

5. To make the icing, put the butter or margarine into a bowl and stir it with a fork. Carry on until it is really creamy.

6. Add some of the icing sugar to the butter and stir it in. Mix in the rest of the icing sugar, a little at a time.

7. Stir the lemon juice or vanilla essence into the mixture. Add a little more if the icing is very thick.

Arrange the cakes into a tree shape, like this.

8. Spread some butter icing on the top of each cake. Use the sweets to make different patterns on each cake.

Use a flaky chocolate bar as a tree trunk.

Wrapping ideas

Tissue twists

1. Cut a square of tissue paper or thin cellophane. Then, put five or six biscuits in the middle of the square.

2. Gather up the edges of the square. Tie a piece of parcel ribbon around the tissue or cellophane, above the gift.

3. Decorate the wrapping with small stickers. You could also try wrapping biscuits with two colours of tissue or cellophane.

Wrapping sweets

Gift boxes filled with sweets and biscuits make great presents.

1. Cut a square of thin cellophane that is bigger than the sweet, like this. Put the sweet in the middle of the square.

Use a tiny piece of tape.

2. Wrap the sweet in the cellophane and tape it. Tie pieces of ribbon around each end of the sweet.

Gift boxes

 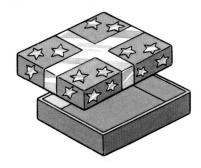 

Paint the inside of a gift box silver or gold. When the paint is dry, fill the box with lots of shredded tissue paper.

Lay a piece of ribbon across the lid and tape it inside. Lay another piece across it. Decorate the lid with stickers.

Cut a piece of tissue paper that is a little bigger than the box. Cut pieces in other colours. Line the box.

Find out how to make gift tags on page 32.

Tags and ribbons

A gift tag

1. Draw a holly leaf shape with a white wax crayon or white candle. Brush bright paint all over the card.

2. Carefully cut around the shape. Write a message on the back. Tape the end of the tag to a present.

Ribbon curls

1. Cut a piece of parcel ribbon 25cm (10in) long. Cut more pieces the same length.

Put your thumb here.

Pull this end.

2. Hold a piece of ribbon between your thumb and the blade of some closed scissors. Pull it firmly.

3. The ribbon curls up. Curl the other pieces of ribbon. Tape them to the middle of a box.